The Daily Danish Challenge

Learn 10 Danish Words a Day for 7 Weeks

Introduction

■ Welcome to "Learn 10 Danish Words a Day for 7 Weeks"! This book is designed to provide an engaging and effective learning experience for children ● and beginners ❤ who are eager to discover the beauty of the Danish language ■. With its carefully curated selection of words and interactive approach ✎, this book aims to make language learning a fun 🎉 and enjoyable journey.

Learning a new language can be both exciting 🎢 and challenging 🧗, but fear not! We have crafted this book with your learning needs in mind. Each day, you will encounter a set of ten Danish words that are carefully chosen to be useful and practical in everyday situations. These words cover various themes ■, allowing you to expand your vocabulary and gain confidence in your language skills.

To facilitate your learning process, we have provided corresponding English ■ words alongside the Danish words, allowing you to establish meaningful connections ■ between the two languages. By actively engaging in writing down (4x) ✎ the correct Danish words, you will reinforce your memory and develop a solid foundation in the language. Embrace the joy of discovery 🌟 as you unlock new words each day, steadily building your language skills one step at a time.

This book is meant to be your companion ■ throughout the course of seven weeks, providing you with a structured learning experience. Each week is carefully planned to introduce new vocabulary 📕 while reinforcing previously learned words, allowing you to review and consolidate your knowledge. Make sure to allocate a few minutes ⏰ each day to engage with the exercises and activities provided. Consistency is key 🔑, and your dedication will yield rewarding results 🏆.

Whether you are a young language enthusiast or a curious beginner, this book is designed to cater to your needs. The vibrant illustrations 🎨 and interactive exercises are intended to spark your imagination and keep you engaged. Remember, learning a language should be an enjoyable experience 🔥, and we hope this book will ignite your passion for Danish.

As you embark on this language learning adventure 🚀, we encourage you to embrace the challenge, celebrate your progress 🎉, and have fun along the way. Learning 10 Danish words a day is an achievable goal, and with perseverance and dedication, you will unlock the doors ▯ to a new world of communication and understanding ●.

Happy learning! ●🎓💬

Attention: The provided English pronunciations of the Danish words are approximations. The actual pronunciation may vary depending on regional accents and dialects in Denmark. Furthermore, some Danish sounds cannot be precisely reproduced in English, meaning that the pronunciations can slightly deviate from the original Danish sounds.

Table of Contents

Week 1

Day 1: Numbers

One	En (uhn)
Two	To (toh)
Three	Tre (treh)
Four	Fire (fee-reh)
Five	Fem (fem)
Six	Seks (seks)
Seven	Syv (soov)
Eight	Otte (ot-teh)
Nine	Ni (nee)
Ten	Ti (tee)

Write the right words down twice on the next page

Six	....	....
Two	....	....
Eight	....	....
Four	....	....
Five	....	....
Eight	....	....
Seven	....	....
Three	....	....
Nine	....	....
Ten	....	....
One	....	....
Two	....	....
Ten	....	....
Four	....	....
Five	....	....
Six	....	....
Seven	....	....
Three	....	....
Nine	....	....
One	....	....

Week 1

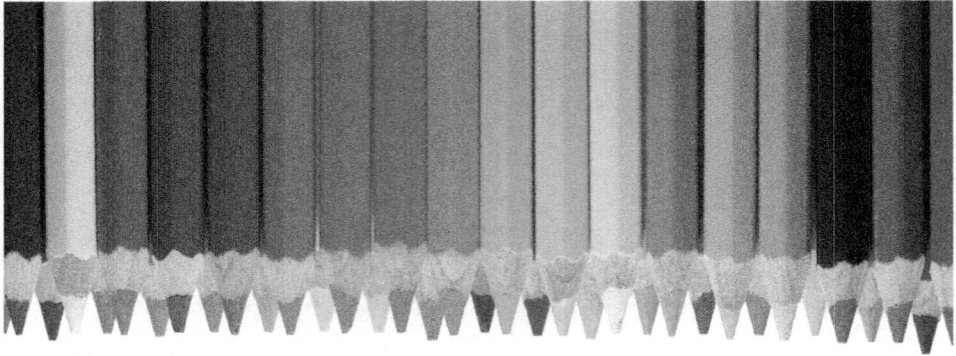

Day 2: Colors

Red	Rød (ruhd)
Blue	Blå (blaw)
Yellow	Gul (gool)
Green	Grøn (grurn)
Orange	Orange (o-runj)
Purple	Lilla (lee-lah)
Pink	Lyserød (loo-seh-ruhd)
Black	Sort (sort)
White	Hvid (veed)
Gray	Grå (graw)

Write the right words down twice on the next page

Red	....	....
Purple	....	....
White	....	....
Gray	....	....
Orange	....	....
Purple	....	....
Blue	....	....
Black	....	....
White	....	....
Gray	....	....
Pink	....	....
Blue	....	....
Yellow	....	....
Green	....	....
Orange	....	....
Pink	....	....
Red	....	....
Black	....	....
Yellow	....	....
Green	....	....

Week 1

Day 3: Family

Mother	Mor (mor)
Father	Far (fahr)
Brother	Bror (broar)
Sister	Søster (soo-ster)
Son	Søn (surn)
Daughter	Datter (daht-ter)
Grandfather	Bedstefar (beds-teh-fahr)
Grandmother	Bedstemor (beds-teh-moar)
Uncle	Onkel (ong-kel)
Aunt	Tante (tan-teh)

Write the right words down twice on the next page

Aunt	....	....
Father	....	....
Mother	....	....
Uncle	....	....
Brother	....	....
Sister	....	....
Son	....	....
Daughter	....	....
Grandfather	....	....
Sister	....	....
Aunt	....	....
Grandmother	....	....
Uncle	....	....
Son	....	....
Grandmother	....	....
Father	....	....
Brother	....	....
Daughter	....	....
Grandfather	....	....
Mother	....	....

Week 1

Day 4: Food

Bread	Brød (bruhrd)
Rice	Ris (rees)
Meat	Kød (kurd)
Vegetables	Grøntsager (grurnt-saher)
Fruit	Frugt (froogt)
Milk	Mælk (melk)
Cheese	Ost (ost)
Eggs	Æg (ai)
Soup	Suppe (soup-peh)
Dessert	Dessert (dess-ert)

Write the right words down twice on the next page

Cheese	....	....
Meat	....	....
Dessert	....	....
Vegetables	....	....
Fruit	....	....
Milk	....	....
Vegetables	....	....
Eggs	....	....
Soup	....	....
Dessert	....	....
Bread	....	....
Rice	....	....
Meat	....	....
Fruit	....	....
Milk	....	....
Cheese	....	....
Bread	....	....
Eggs	....	....
Soup	....	....
Rice	....	....

Week 1

Day 5: Animals

Dog	Hund (hoond)
Cat	Kat (kaht)
Lion	Løve (luh-veh)
Sheep	Får (fawr)
Pig	Gris (greez)
Monkey	Abekat (ah-beh-kaht)
Tiger	Tiger (tee-gehr)
Bear	Bjørn (byurn)
Horse	Hest (hest)
Bird	Fugl (fool)

Write the right words down twice on the next page

Monkey	....	....
Cat	....	....
Bird	....	....
Lion	....	....
Sheep	....	....
Pig	....	....
Monkey	....	....
Tiger	....	....
Bear	....	....
Horse	....	....
Bird	....	....
Dog	....	....
Cat	....	....
Lion	....	....
Sheep	....	....
Pig	....	....
Horse	....	....
Tiger	....	....
Bear	....	....
Dog	....	....

Week 1

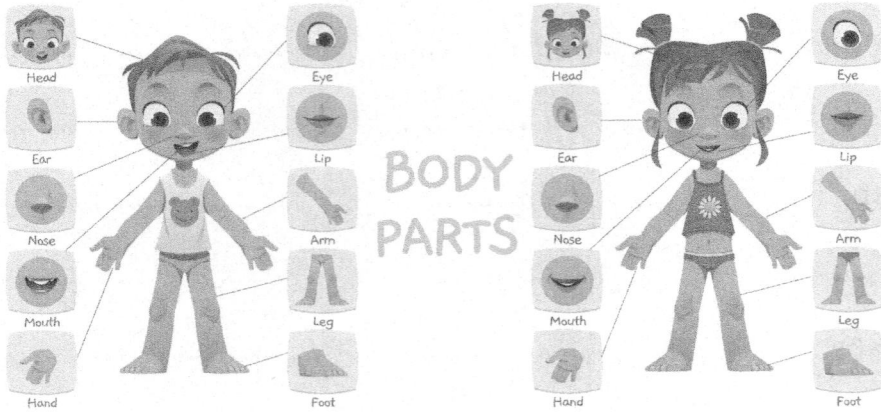

BODY PARTS

Day 6: Body

Head	Hoved (hoh-ved)
Neck	Nakke (nah-keh)
Belly	Mave (mah-veh)
Shoulder	Skulder (skool-der)
Knee	Knæ (knai)
Back	Ryg (ryg)
Arms	Arme (ar-meh)
Hands	Hænder (hen-der)
Legs	Ben (ben)
Feet	Fødder (fuh-der)

Write the right words down twice on the next page

Shoulder	....	....
Back	....	....
Feet	....	....
Belly	....	....
Hands	....	....
Shoulder	....	....
Knee	....	....
Back	....	....
Arms	....	....
Hands	....	....
Neck	....	....
Feet	....	....
Head	....	....
Neck	....	....
Belly	....	....
Knee	....	....
Legs	....	....
Arms	....	....
Head	....	....
Legs	....	....

Week 1

Day 7: Weather

Sun	Sol (sole)
Rain	Regn (rain)
Cloud	Sky (skoo)
Wind	Vind (vind)
Snow	Sne (sneh)
Thunder	Torden (tor-den)
Lightning	Lyn (loon)
Storm	Storm (storm)
Fog	Tåge (taw-geh)
Rainbow	Regnbue (rain-buh)

Write the right words down twice on the next page

Storm	....	....
Rain	....	....
Fog	....	....
Snow	....	....
Cloud	....	....
Wind	....	....
Snow	....	....
Thunder	....	....
Rain	....	....
Lightning	....	....
Storm	....	....
Fog	....	....
Rainbow	....	....
Sun	....	....
Cloud	....	....
Wind	....	....
Thunder	....	....
Lightning	....	....
Rainbow	....	....
Sun	....	....

Week 2

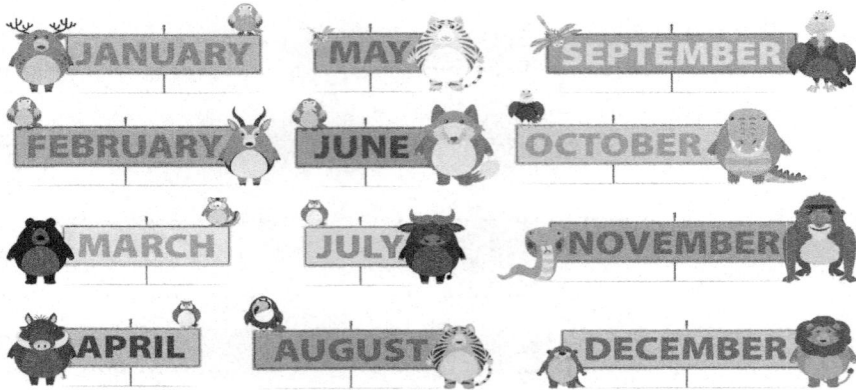

Day 8: Months

January	Januar (yan-oo-ar)
February	Februar (feb-oo-ar)
March	Marts (marts)
April	April (ah-preel)
May	Maj (mai)
June	Juni (yoo-nee)
July	Juli (yoo-lee)
August	August (ow-gust)
September	September (sep-tem-ber)
October	Oktober (ok-toh-ber)

Write the right words down twice on the next page

20

October	....	....
February	....	....
August	....	....
October	....	....
April	....	....
May	....	....
June	....	....
August	....	....
March	....	....
September	....	....
May	....	....
January	....	....
July	....	....
March	....	....
April	....	....
June	....	....
January	....	....
July	....	....
February	....	....
September	....	....

Week 2

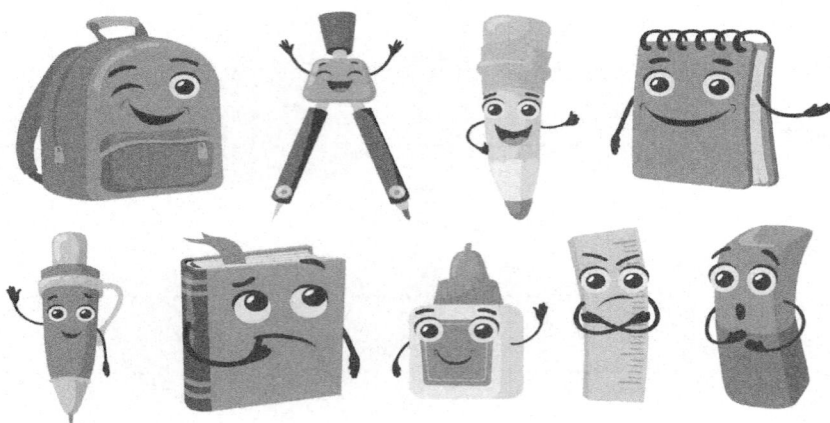

Day 9: School

Teacher	Lærer (lae-rer)
Student	Studerende (stoo-der-en-deh)
Classroom	Klasseværelse (klas-seh-vair-el-seh)
Book	Bog (bohg)
Pen	Pen (pen)
Pencil	Blyant (blee-ant)
Desk	Skrivebord (skree-veh-bord)
Chair	Stol (stohl)
Homework	Hjemmearbejde (yem-meh-ar-bei-deh)
Exam	Eksamen (eks-ah-men)

Write the right words down twice on the next page

Chair	....	....
Homework	....	....
Teacher	....	....
Student	....	....
Classroom	....	....
Exam	....	....
Pen	....	....
Pencil	....	....
Desk	....	....
Classroom	....	....
Homework	....	....
Exam	....	....
Teacher	....	....
Student	....	....
Desk	....	....
Book	....	....
Pen	....	....
Pencil	....	....
Chair	....	....
Book	....	....

Week 2

Day 10: Transportation

Car	Bil (bil)
Bus	Bus (boos)
Train	Tog (tohg)
Bicycle	Cykel (soo-kel)
Motorcycle	Motorcykel (moh-tor-soo-kel)
Boat	Båd (bawd)
Airplane	Fly (flee)
Helicopter	Helikopter (heh-lee-kop-ter)
Truck	Lastbil (las-bil)
Metro	Metro (meh-tro)

Write the right words down twice on the next page

Airplane	....	....
Bus	....	....
Train	....	....
Metro	....	....
Truck	....	....
Motorcycle	....	....
Boat	....	....
Airplane	....	....
Helicopter	....	....
Truck	....	....
Metro	....	....
Car	....	....
Bus	....	....
Train	....	....
Bicycle	....	....
Helicopter	....	....
Motorcycle	....	....
Boat	....	....
Bicycle	....	....
Car	....	....

Week 2

Day 11: Clothing

Shirt	Skjorte (skyor-teh)
Pants	Bukser (book-ser)
Dress	Kjole (cho-leh)
Skirt	Nederdel (nay-der-del)
Jacket	Jakke (yak-keh)
Shoes	Sko (skoh)
Socks	Sokker (sok-ker)
Hat	Hat (haht)
Gloves	Handsker (hands-ker)
Scarf	Tørklæde (tur-klai-deh)

Write the right words down twice on the next page

Socks	....	....
Pants	....	....
Dress	....	....
Jacket	....	....
Skirt	....	....
Scarf	....	....
Shoes	....	....
Socks	....	....
Hat	....	....
Gloves	....	....
Scarf	....	....
Shirt	....	....
Pants	....	....
Dress	....	....
Skirt	....	....
Jacket	....	....
Shoes	....	....
Gloves	....	....
Hat	....	....
Shirt	....	....

Week 2

Day 12: Emotions

Happy	Glad (glad)
Sad	Trist (trist)
Angry	Vred (vred)
Excited	Spændt (spanned)
Surprised	Overrasket (o-ver-ra-sket)
Scared	Bange (ban-geh)
Nervous	Nervøs (ner-voos)
Bored	Ked (ked)
Confused	Forvirret (for-vir-red)
Calm	Rolig (ro-lig)

Write the right words down twice on the next page

Confused   ....

Happy   ....

Calm   ....

Surprised   ....

Sad   ....

Angry   ....

Excited   ....

Nervous   ....

Scared   ....

Nervous   ....

Bored   ....

Scared   ....

Calm   ....

Happy   ....

Sad   ....

Bored   ....

Angry   ....

Excited   ....

Surprised   ....

Confused   ....

Week 2

Day 13: Hobbies

Reading	Læsning (les-ning)
Painting	Maleri (ma-leri)
Singing	Sang (sang)
Dancing	Dans (dans)
Cooking	Madlavning (mad-lav-ning)
Photography	Fotografering (fo-to-gra-fe-ring)
Sleeping	Søvn (surn)
Writing	Skrivning (skriv-ning)
Gardening	Havearbejde (hav-ar-bai-deh)
Sports	Sport (sport)

Write the right words down twice on the next page

Gardening	....	....
Painting	....	....
Photography	....	....
Painting	....	....
Dancing	....	....
Cooking	....	....
Photography	....	....
Sports	....	....
Writing	....	....
Gardening	....	....
Sports	....	....
Reading	....	....
Sleeping	....	....
Singing	....	....
Dancing	....	....
Cooking	....	....
Singing	....	....
Sleeping	....	....
Writing	....	....
Reading	....	....

Week 2

Day 14: Sports

Football	Fodbold (fud-bold)
Basketball	Basketball (bas-ket-ball)
Tennis	Tennis (ten-nis)
Swimming	Svømning (svm-ning)
Volleyball	Volleyball (vol-ley-ball)
Golf	Golf (golf)
Cycling	Cykling (soo-kling)
Running	Løb (lurb)
Fitness	Fitness (fit-ness)
Martial arts	Kampsport (kamp-sport)

Write the right words down twice on the next page

Swimming	....	....
Football	....	....
Fitness	....	....
Basketball	....	....
Golf	....	....
Swimming	....	....
Volleyball	....	....
Golf	....	....
Running	....	....
Cycling	....	....
Running	....	....
Fitness	....	....
Martial arts	....	....
Football	....	....
Basketball	....	....
Tennis	....	....
Martial arts	....	....
Volleyball	....	....
Cycling	....	....
Tennis	....	....

Week 3

Day 15: Nature

Tree	Træ (trai)
Flower	Blomst (blomst)
River	Flod (flod)
Mountain	Bjerg (byerg)
Lake	Sø (soo)
Beach	Strand (strand)
Forest	Skov (skov)
Grass	Græs (grahs)
Star	Stjerne (styern-neh)
Cloud	Sky (skoo)

Write the right words down twice on the next page

Grass	....	....
Beach	....	....
Mountain	....	....
Cloud	....	....
Flower	....	....
River	....	....
Mountain	....	....
Lake	....	....
Beach	....	....
Forest	....	....
Grass	....	....
Star	....	....
Forest	....	....
Cloud	....	....
Tree	....	....
Flower	....	....
River	....	....
Star	....	....
Lake	....	....
Tree	....	....

Week 3

🐕	Monday	🐦	Thursday
🐒	Tuesday	🐘	**Friday**
🐈	Wednesday	🐷	**Saturday**
		🐓	Sunday

Day 16: Days of the Week

Monday	Mandag (man-day)
Tuesday	Tirsdag (tirs-day)
Wednesday	Onsdag (ons-day)
Thursday	Torsdag (tors-day)
Friday	Fredag (fre-day)
Saturday	Lørdag (lur-day)
Sunday	Søndag (sun-day)
Yesterday	I går (i yawr)
Tomorrow	I morgen (i mor-gen)
Today	I dag (i day)

Write the right words down twice on the next page

Sunday	....	....
Tuesday	....	....
Saturday	....	....
Today	....	....
Wednesday	....	....
Tomorrow	....	....
Friday	....	....
Saturday	....	....
Yesterday	....	....
Tomorrow	....	....
Today	....	....
Monday	....	....
Thursday	....	....
Wednesday	....	....
Thursday	....	....
Friday	....	....
Monday	....	....
Sunday	....	....
Yesterday	....	....
Tuesday	....	....

Week 3

Day 17: Music

Song	Sang (sang)
Melody	Melodi (me-lo-dee)
Rhythm	Rytme (rutmeh)
Instrument	Instrument (ins-tru-ment)
Singing	Syngende (sun-gen-de)
Band	Orkester (or-kes-ter)
Concert	Koncert (kon-sert)
Piano	Klaver (klah-ver)
Guitar	Guitar (gi-tar)
Sound	Lyd (lood)

Write the right words down twice on the next page

Concert	....	....
Melody	....	....
Rhythm	....	....
Sound	....	....
Guitar	....	....
Piano	....	....
Instrument	....	....
Singing	....	....
Band	....	....
Piano	....	....
Guitar	....	....
Sound	....	....
Song	....	....
Rhythm	....	....
Instrument	....	....
Singing	....	....
Band	....	....
Concert	....	....
Song	....	....
Melody	....	....

Week 3

Day 18: Jobs

Teacher	Lærer (lae-rer)
Doctor	Læge (lae-geh)
Engineer	Ingeniør (in-ge-nyor)
Chef	Kok (kok)
Police officer	Politibetjent (poli-ti-betyent)
Firefighter	Brandmand (brand-mand)
Nurse	Sygeplejerske (see-ge-ple-yerske)
Pilot	Pilot (pee-lot)
Lawyer	Advokat (ad-vokat)
Artist	Kunstner (koonst-ner)

Write the right words down twice on the next page

Lawyer	....	....
Teacher	....	....
Chef	....	....
Doctor	....	....
Engineer	....	....
Chef	....	....
Police officer	....	....
Pilot	....	....
Nurse	....	....
Doctor	....	....
Artist	....	....
Teacher	....	....
Pilot	....	....
Engineer	....	....
Artist	....	....
Police officer	....	....
Firefighter	....	....
Nurse	....	....
Lawyer	....	....
Firefighter	....	....

Week 3

Day 19: Fruits

Apple	Æble (able)
Banana	Banan (ba-nan)
Orange	Appelsin (ap-pel-sin)
Strawberry	Jordbær (yor-bair)
Grapes	Druer (droo-er)
Watermelon	Vandmelon (vand-mel-on)
Pineapple	Ananas (a-nan-as)
Mango	Mango (man-go)
Kiwi	Kiwi (ki-vee)
Peach	Fersken (fers-ken)

Write the right words down twice on the next page

Orange ....

Apple ....

Banana ....

Orange ....

Mango ....

Grapes ....

Kiwi ....

Pineapple ....

Mango ....

Peach ....

Apple ....

Banana ....

Strawberry ....

Grapes ....

Watermelon ....

Pineapple ....

Kiwi ....

Strawberry ....

Peach ....

Watermelon ....

Week 3

Day 20: Vegetables

Carrot	Gulerod (gool-er-od)
Tomato	Tomat (to-mat)
Potato	Kartoffel (kar-tofel)
Onion	Løg (lurg)
Cucumber	Agurk (a-gurk)
Broccoli	Broccoli (bro-kol-lee)
Spinach	Spinat (spi-naht)
Corn	Majs (mais)
Cabbage	Kål (kawl)
Mushroom	Svamp (svamp)

Write the right words down twice on the next page

Corn	....	....
Tomato	....	....
Potato	....	....
Mushroom	....	....
Spinach	....	....
Onion	....	....
Broccoli	....	....
Spinach	....	....
Corn	....	....
Tomato	....	....
Mushroom	....	....
Carrot	....	....
Cucumber	....	....
Potato	....	....
Onion	....	....
Cucumber	....	....
Cabbage	....	....
Carrot	....	....
Cabbage	....	....
Broccoli	....	....

Week 3

Day 21: Tools

Hammer	Hammer (ham-mer)
Screwdriver	Skrue (skroo-eh)
Wrench	Nøgle (nur-gleh)
Pliers	Tang (tang)
Saw	Save (sa-veh)
Drill	Boremaskine (bo-reh-mas-ki-ne)
Tape measure	Målebånd (mawl-eh-bawnd)
Chisel	Mejsel (mais-el)
Level	Skovl (skovl)
Paintbrush	Malerpensel (ma-ler-pen-sel)

Write the right words down twice on the next page

Level	....	....
Screwdriver	....	....
Wrench	....	....
Paintbrush	....	....
Pliers	....	....
Drill	....	....
Chisel	....	....
Level	....	....
Paintbrush	....	....
Hammer	....	....
Screwdriver	....	....
Pliers	....	....
Saw	....	....
Drill	....	....
Tape measure	....	....
Hammer	....	....
Wrench	....	....
Saw	....	....
Chisel	....	....
Tape measure	....	....

Week 4

Day 22: Kitchen

Plate	Tallerken (tal-ler-ken)
Fork	Gaffel (gaf-fel)
Knife	Kniv (knif)
Spoon	Ske (skeh)
Cup	Kop (kop)
Bowl	Skål (skawl)
Pan	Pande (pan-deh)
Pot	Gryde (gry-deh)
Cutting board	Skærebræt (skai-reh-bret)
Oven	Ovn (ovn)

Write the right words down twice on the next page

Plate	....	....
Oven	....	....
Fork	....	....
Bowl	....	....
Knife	....	....
Spoon	....	....
Cup	....	....
Cutting board	....	....
Knife	....	....
Fork	....	....
Bowl	....	....
Spoon	....	....
Pan	....	....
Pot	....	....
Cutting board	....	....
Oven	....	....
Pot	....	....
Plate	....	....
Cup	....	....
Pan	....	....

Week 4

Day 23: Instruments

Guitar	Guitar (gi-tar)
Piano	Klaver (klah-ver)
Violin	Violin (vee-o-lin)
Flute	Fløjte (floy-teh)
Trumpet	Trompet (trom-pet)
Drum	Tromme (trom-meh)
Saxophone	Saxofon (sax-o-fon)
Cello	Cello (tchel-lo)
Clarinet	Klarinet (klar-i-net)
Harp	Harpe (har-peh)

Write the right words down twice on the next page

Flute ....

Piano ....

Trumpet ....

Violin ....

Cello ....

Trumpet ....

Drum ....

Saxophone ....

Cello ....

Clarinet ....

Violin ....

Saxophone ....

Harp ....

Guitar ....

Drum ....

Piano ....

Harp ....

Flute ....

Guitar ....

Clarinet ....

Week 4

Day 24: Buildings

House	Hus (hoos)
School	Skole (sko-leh)
Hospital	Hospital (hos-pi-tal)
Library	Bibliotek (bib-lee-o-tek)
Bank	Bank (bank)
Restaurant	Restaurant (res-tau-rant)
Hotel	Hotel (ho-tel)
Museum	Museum (mu-se-um)
Church	Kirke (kir-keh)
Stadium	Stadion (sta-dee-on)

Write the right words down twice on the next page

Hospital	....	....
House	....	....
Museum	....	....
School	....	....
Stadium	....	....
Hospital	....	....
Church	....	....
Restaurant	....	....
Hotel	....	....
Museum	....	....
Church	....	....
House	....	....
School	....	....
Library	....	....
Bank	....	....
Restaurant	....	....
Hotel	....	....
Library	....	....
Bank	....	....
Stadium	....	....

Week 4

Day 25: Directions

Left	Venstre (ven-streh)
Right	Højre (hoi-reh)
Straight	Ligeud (lee-gowd)
Up	Op (op)
Down	Ned (ned)
North	Nord (nord)
South	Syd (syd)
East	Øst (urst)
West	Vest (vest)
Stop	Stop (stop)

Write the right words down twice on the next page

Straight	....	....
Left	....	....
South	....	....
Straight	....	....
Up	....	....
Down	....	....
North	....	....
Stop	....	....
East	....	....
Stop	....	....
Left	....	....
Right	....	....
South	....	....
Right	....	....
North	....	....
West	....	....
Up	....	....
Down	....	....
East	....	....
West	....	....

Week 4

Day 26: Bedroom

Bed	Seng (seng)
Pillow	Pude (poo-deh)
Blanket	Tæppe (taep-peh)
Wardrobe	Garderobe (gar-de-robe)
Nightstand	Natbord (nat-bord)
Lamp	Lampe (lump-eh)
Alarm clock	Vækkeur (vaek-ur)
Dresser	Kommode (kom-mo-de)
Hanger	Bøjle (boi-le)
Mirror	Spejl (spaigel)

Write the right words down twice on the next page

Hanger	....	....
Pillow	....	....
Dresser	....	....
Wardrobe	....	....
Mirror	....	....
Nightstand	....	....
Lamp	....	....
Alarm clock	....	....
Dresser	....	....
Blanket	....	....
Hanger	....	....
Mirror	....	....
Wardrobe	....	....
Nightstand	....	....
Bed	....	....
Blanket	....	....
Lamp	....	....
Bed	....	....
Alarm clock	....	....
Pillow	....	....

Week 4

Day 27: Countries

United States	Forenede Stater (fo-ren-eh-de sta-ter)
United Kingdom	Storbritannien (stor-bri-tan-ien)
Canada	Canada (ca-na-da)
Australia	Australien (aus-tra-li-en)
Germany	Tyskland (tysk-land)
France	Frankrig (frank-rig)
China	Kina (ki-na)
Japan	Japan (ya-pan)
Brazil	Brasilien (bra-sil-i-en)
India	Indien (in-di-en)

Write the right words down twice on the next page

China	....	....
United States	....	....
India	....	....
Canada	....	....
Australia	....	....
Brazil	....	....
China	....	....
Japan	....	....
Brazil	....	....
India	....	....
United States	....	....
Germany	....	....
Canada	....	....
Australia	....	....
Japan	....	....
United Kingdom	....	....
Germany	....	....
France	....	....
United Kingdom	....	....
France	....	....

Week 4

Day 28: Travel

Airport	Lufthavn (loof-thawn)
Passport	Pas (pas)
Ticket	Billet (bil-let)
Suitcase	Kuffert (kuf-fert)
Hotel	Hotel (ho-tel)
Sightseeing	Sightseeing (site-se-ing)
Beach	Strand (strand)
Adventure	Eventyr (ev-en-teer)
Map	Kort (kort)
Tourist	Turist (too-rist)

Write the right words down twice on the next page

Airport	....	....
Adventure	....	....
Passport	....	....
Ticket	....	....
Suitcase	....	....
Hotel	....	....
Sightseeing	....	....
Beach	....	....
Adventure	....	....
Map	....	....
Tourist	....	....
Airport	....	....
Passport	....	....
Ticket	....	....
Suitcase	....	....
Hotel	....	....
Sightseeing	....	....
Beach	....	....
Map	....	....
Tourist	....	....

Week 5

Day 29: Health

Doctor	Læge (lae-geh)
Hospital	Hospital (hos-pi-tal)
Medicine	Medicin (me-di-sin)
Nurse	Sygeplejerske (see-ge-ple-yerske)
Pain	Smerte (smehr-teh)
Appointment	Aftale (af-ta-le)
Exercise	Motion (mo-tion)
Sleep	Søvn (surn)
Diet	Kost (kost)
Vitamin	Vitamin (vi-ta-min)

Write the right words down twice on the next page

Appointment	....	....
Vitamin	....	....
Hospital	....	....
Medicine	....	....
Nurse	....	....
Pain	....	....
Sleep	....	....
Hospital	....	....
Exercise	....	....
Nurse	....	....
Sleep	....	....
Diet	....	....
Vitamin	....	....
Doctor	....	....
Pain	....	....
Appointment	....	....
Exercise	....	....
Doctor	....	....
Medicine	....	....
Diet	....	....

Week 5

Day 30: Languages

English	Engelsk (eng-elsk)
Spanish	Spansk (span-sk)
French	Fransk (fransk)
German	Tysk (tysk)
Dutch	Hollandsk (hol-lan-sk)
Frisian	Frisisk (fri-sisk)
Russian	Russisk (rus-sisk)
Portuguese	Portugisisk (por-tu-gi-sisk)
Japanese	Japansk (ya-pan-sk)
Italian	Italiensk (it-a-li-ensk)

Write the right words down twice on the next page

German ....

Spanish ....

Portuguese ....

French ....

German ....

Dutch ....

Frisian ....

Russian ....

Italian ....

Russian ....

Japanese ....

Frisian ....

English ....

Italian ....

English ....

Spanish ....

French ....

Dutch ....

Portuguese ....

Japanese ....

Week 5

Day 31: Church

Priest	Præst (praest)
Worship	Dyrkelse (dyrk-el-se)
Prayer	Bøn (boon)
Bible	Bibelen (bee-be-len)
Sermon	Prædiken (praed-i-ken)
Choir	Kor (kor)
Altar	Alter (al-ter)
Cross	Kors (kors)
Faith	Tro (tro)
Ceremony	Ceremoni (ce-re-mo-ni)

Write the right words down twice on the next page

Choir	....	....
Worship	....	....
Altar	....	....
Bible	....	....
Ceremony	....	....
Faith	....	....
Sermon	....	....
Choir	....	....
Altar	....	....
Cross	....	....
Faith	....	....
Ceremony	....	....
Cross	....	....
Priest	....	....
Worship	....	....
Prayer	....	....
Bible	....	....
Sermon	....	....
Priest	....	....
Prayer	....	....

Week 5

Day 32: Birds

Eagle	Ørn (urn)
Sparrow	Spurv (spurv)
Owl	Ugle (oog-le)
Parrot	Papegøje (pa-pe-goi-eh)
Hummingbird	Kolibri (ko-li-bri)
Pigeon	Due (doo-eh)
Flamingo	Flamingo (fla-min-go)
Swan	Svane (sva-ne)
Peacock	Påfugl (paw-fool)
Duck	And (and)

Write the right words down twice on the next page

Duck ....

Eagle ....

Sparrow ....

Owl ....

Eagle ....

Swan ....

Sparrow ....

Flamingo ....

Hummingbird ....

Pigeon ....

Flamingo ....

Owl ....

Swan ....

Peacock ....

Duck ....

Parrot ....

Hummingbird ....

Pigeon ....

Parrot ....

Peacock ....

Week 5

Day 33: Science

Chemistry	Kemi (ke-mi)
Biology	Biologi (bio-lo-gi)
Physics	Fysik (fy-sik)
Astronomy	Astronomi (as-tro-no-mi)
Experiment	Eksperiment (eks-per-i-ment)
Laboratory	Laboratorium (la-bo-ra-to-rium)
Microscope	Mikroskop (mi-kro-skop)
Hypothesis	Hypotese (hy-po-te-se)
Scientist	Forsker (for-sker)
Discovery	Opdagelse (op-da-gel-se)

Write the right words down twice on the next page

Hypothesis	....	....
Biology	....	....
Experiment	....	....
Astronomy	....	....
Physics	....	....
Astronomy	....	....
Microscope	....	....
Scientist	....	....
Laboratory	....	....
Physics	....	....
Microscope	....	....
Hypothesis	....	....
Chemistry	....	....
Scientist	....	....
Discovery	....	....
Chemistry	....	....
Biology	....	....
Laboratory	....	....
Discovery	....	....
Experiment	....	....

Week 5

Day 34: Film

Actor	Skuespiller (skoo-es-pil-ler)
Actress	Skuespillerinde (skoo-es-pil-lin-de)
Director	Instruktør (in-struk-toer)
Script	Manuskript (ma-nus-kript)
Camera	Kamera (ka-mer-a)
Scene	Scene (se-ne)
Drama	Drama (dra-ma)
Comedy	Komedi (ko-me-di)
Action	Action (ak-tion)
Television	Fjernsyn (fjern-syn)

Write the right words down twice on the next page

Actor	....	....
Camera	....	....
Action	....	....
Director	....	....
Script	....	....
Television	....	....
Camera	....	....
Scene	....	....
Drama	....	....
Comedy	....	....
Action	....	....
Television	....	....
Actor	....	....
Actress	....	....
Director	....	....
Scene	....	....
Actress	....	....
Drama	....	....
Comedy	....	....
Script	....	....

Week 5

Day 35: History

Ancient	Gamle (gam-le)
Civilization	Civilisation (si-vil-i-sa-tion)
Emperor	Kejser (kai-ser)
Revolution	Revolution (re-vo-lu-tion)
War	Krig (krig)
Kingdom	Kongerige (kon-ge-ri-ge)
Archaeology	Arkæologi (ar-kai-o-lo-gi)
Renaissance	Renæssance (re-nae-ssan-ce)
Independence	Uafhængighed (u-af-hen-ge-hed)
Event	Begivenhed (be-giv-en-hed)

Write the right words down twice on the next page

Kingdom	....	....
Event	....	....
Archaeology	....	....
Emperor	....	....
Renaissance	....	....
Independence	....	....
Revolution	....	....
War	....	....
Kingdom	....	....
Archaeology	....	....
Renaissance	....	....
Independence	....	....
Event	....	....
Ancient	....	....
Civilization	....	....
Emperor	....	....
Revolution	....	....
War	....	....
Ancient	....	....
Civilization	....	....

Week 6

Day 36: Drinks

Water	Vand (vand)
Coffee	Kaffe (kaf-fe)
Tea	Te (te)
Juice	Juice (yoo-se)
Soda	Sodavand (so-da-vand)
Milk	Mælk (melk)
Wine	Vin (vin)
Beer	Øl (url)
Cocktail	Cocktail (cock-tail)
Lemonade	Limonade (li-mo-na-de)

Write the right words down twice on the next page

Soda	....	....
Cocktail	....	....
Tea	....	....
Juice	....	....
Wine	....	....
Soda	....	....
Milk	....	....
Wine	....	....
Beer	....	....
Cocktail	....	....
Lemonade	....	....
Water	....	....
Coffee	....	....
Water	....	....
Tea	....	....
Lemonade	....	....
Juice	....	....
Milk	....	....
Coffee	....	....
Beer	....	....

Week 6

Day 37: Business

Entrepreneur	Iværksætter (i-vairk-setter)
Company	Virksomhed (virks-om-hed)
Marketing	Marketing (market-ing)
Sales	Salg (salg)
Product	Produkt (pro-dukt)
Customer	Kunde (kun-de)
Finance	Finansiering (fi-nan-see-ring)
Strategy	Strategi (stra-te-gi)
Profit	Profit (pro-fit)
Investment	Investering (in-ves-te-ring)

Write the right words down twice on the next page

Strategy	....	....
Company	....	....
Marketing	....	....
Sales	....	....
Product	....	....
Customer	....	....
Finance	....	....
Investment	....	....
Customer	....	....
Profit	....	....
Finance	....	....
Investment	....	....
Entrepreneur	....	....
Company	....	....
Marketing	....	....
Sales	....	....
Product	....	....
Profit	....	....
Entrepreneur	....	....
Strategy	....	....

Week 6

Day 38: Beach

Sand	Sand (sand)
Waves	Bølger (bøl-ger)
Sunscreen	Solcreme (sol-krem-e)
Swim	Svømme (svum-me)
Seashells	Skaller (skal-ler)
Umbrella	Paraply (pa-ra-ply)
Beach ball	Strandbold (strand-bold)
Sunbathing	Solbade (sol-ba-de)
Surfing	Surfing (surf-ing)
Picnic	Picnic (pic-nic)

Write the right words down twice on the next page

Beach ball	....	....
Sunbathing	....	....
Waves	....	....
Sunscreen	....	....
Picnic	....	....
Swim	....	....
Umbrella	....	....
Beach ball	....	....
Picnic	....	....
Sand	....	....
Sunscreen	....	....
Swim	....	....
Seashells	....	....
Surfing	....	....
Waves	....	....
Umbrella	....	....
Seashells	....	....
Sunbathing	....	....
Surfing	....	....
Sand	....	....

Week 6

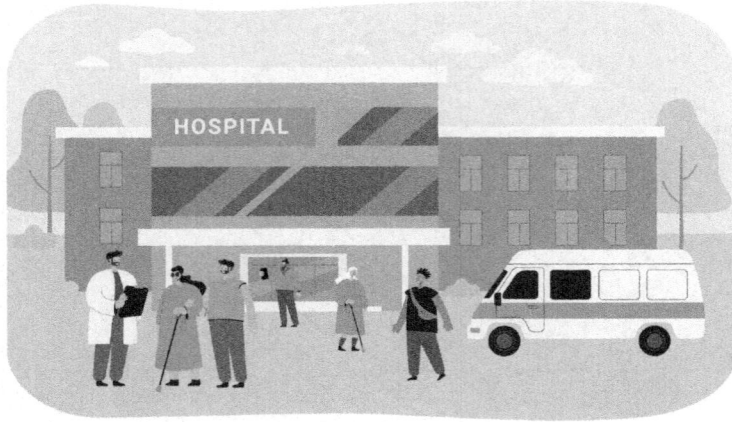

Day 39: Hospital

Doctor	Læge (lae-geh)
Nurse	Sygeplejerske (see-ge-ple-yerske)
Patient	Patient (pa-tient)
Emergency	Nødsituation (nurd-si-tu-a-tion)
Surgery	Operation (ope-ra-tion)
Appointment	Aftale (af-ta-le)
Stethoscope	Stetoskop (ste-to-skop)
X-ray	Røntgen (rurn-gen)
Medicine	Medicin (me-di-sin)
Recovery	Genopretning (gen-op-ret-ning)

Write the right words down twice on the next page

Nurse ....

Doctor ....

Appointment ....

Stethoscope ....

Emergency ....

Recovery ....

Nurse ....

Patient ....

Emergency ....

Surgery ....

Appointment ....

Stethoscope ....

X-ray ....

Medicine ....

Recovery ....

Doctor ....

Surgery ....

Patient ....

X-ray ....

Medicine ....

Week 6

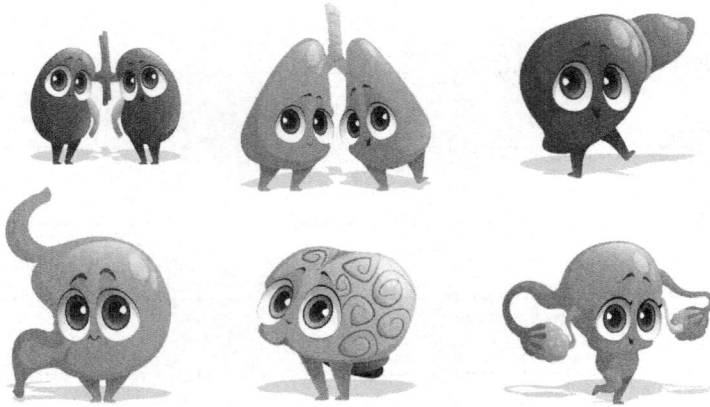

Day 40: Internal Body

Heart	Hjerte (yehr-te)
Lungs	Lunger (lun-ger)
Stomach	Mave (ma-ve)
Liver	Lever (le-ver)
Kidneys	Nyrer (nyr-er)
Brain	Hjerne (hyer-ne)
Intestines	Tarme (tar-me)
Bladder	Blære (blai-re)
Bones	Knogler (knog-ler)
Muscles	Muskler (mus-klar)

Write the right words down twice on the next page

Kidneys ....

Stomach ....

Heart ....

Intestines ....

Brain ....

Lungs ....

Stomach ....

Liver ....

Muscles ....

Kidneys ....

Intestines ....

Bladder ....

Bones ....

Muscles ....

Heart ....

Lungs ....

Bones ....

Liver ....

Brain ....

Bladder ....

Week 6

Day 41: Internet

Website	Hjemmeside (yem-me-side)
Email	E-mail (e-mail)
Social media	Sociale medier (so-ci-a-le me-di-er)
Online shopping	Online shopping (on-line shop-ping)
Search engine	Søgemaskine (soe-ge-ma-ski-ne)
Password	Adgangskode (ad-gang-kode)
Wi-Fi	Wi-Fi (wi-fi)
Download	Download (down-load)
Upload	Upload (up-load)
Browser	Browser (browser)

Write the right words down twice on the next page

Browser	....	....
Website	....	....
Email	....	....
Social media	....	....
Wi-Fi	....	....
Search engine	....	....
Password	....	....
Wi-Fi	....	....
Download	....	....
Upload	....	....
Browser	....	....
Online shopping	....	....
Email	....	....
Social media	....	....
Online shopping	....	....
Password	....	....
Website	....	....
Download	....	....
Upload	....	....
Search engine	....	....

Week 6

Day 42: Shapes

Cirkel	Cirkel (sir-kel)
Square	Firkant (fir-kant)
Rectangle	Rektangel (rek-tan-gel)
Triangle	Trekant (tre-kant)
Oval	Oval (o-val)
Pyramid	Pyramide (py-ra-mi-de)
Cube	Kube (ku-be)
Arrow	Pil (pil)
Star	Stjerne (styer-ne)
Cylinder	Cylinder (cy-lin-der)

Write the right words down twice on the next page

Rectangle	....	....
Triangle	....	....
Pyramid	....	....
Arrow	....	....
Star	....	....
Cylinder	....	....
Oval	....	....
Square	....	....
Star	....	....
Cube	....	....
Cirkel	....	....
Pyramid	....	....
Cylinder	....	....
Cirkel	....	....
Square	....	....
Rectangle	....	....
Triangle	....	....
Oval	....	....
Cube	....	....
Arrow	....	....

Week 7

Day 43: House Parts

Roof	Tag (tag)
Door	Dør (dør)
Window	Vindue (vin-du-e)
Floor	Gulv (gulv)
Wall	Væg (vai-g)
Ceiling	Loft (loft)
Stairs	Trapper (trap-per)
Bathroom	Badeværelse (ba-de-vai-rel-se)
Kitchen	Køkken (køk-ken)
Bedroom	Soveværelse (so-ve-vai-rel-se)

Write the right words down twice on the next page

Wall	....	....
Door	....	....
Stairs	....	....
Ceiling	....	....
Floor	....	....
Wall	....	....
Ceiling	....	....
Bedroom	....	....
Stairs	....	....
Bathroom	....	....
Kitchen	....	....
Bedroom	....	....
Roof	....	....
Door	....	....
Window	....	....
Floor	....	....
Roof	....	....
Bathroom	....	....
Kitchen	....	....
Window	....	....

Week 7

Day 44: Around the House

Plant	Plante (plan-te)
Watering can	Vandkande (vand-kan-de)
Shed	Skur (skur)
Doorbell	Dørklokke (dør-klok-ke)
Fence	Hegn (hegn)
Mailbox	Postkasse (post-kas-se)
Lawn mower	Græsslåmaskine (grass-law-ma-ski-ne)
Wheelbarrow	Trillebør (tril-le-bør)
Shovel	Skovl (skovl)
Bench	Bænk (baink)

Write the right words down twice on the next page

Watering can ....

Shed ....

Doorbell ....

Mailbox ....

Bench ....

Fence ....

Wheelbarrow ....

Shed ....

Mailbox ....

Bench ....

Lawn mower ....

Wheelbarrow ....

Shovel ....

Plant ....

Watering can ....

Doorbell ....

Fence ....

Lawn mower ....

Shovel ....

Plant ....

Week 7

Day 45: Face

Eyes	Øjne (øyn-e)
Nose	Næse (nai-se)
Mouth	Mund (mund)
Ears	Ører (ør-er)
Cheeks	Kindben (kind-ben)
Forehead	Pande (pan-de)
Chin	Hage (ha-ge)
Lips	Læber (lai-ber)
Teeth	Tænder (tæn-der)
Eyebrows	Øjenbryn (ø-jen-bryn)

Write the right words down twice on the next page

Eyebrows	....	....
Nose	....	....
Chin	....	....
Forehead	....	....
Ears	....	....
Cheeks	....	....
Forehead	....	....
Chin	....	....
Nose	....	....
Lips	....	....
Teeth	....	....
Eyebrows	....	....
Eyes	....	....
Lips	....	....
Teeth	....	....
Mouth	....	....
Ears	....	....
Mouth	....	....
Cheeks	....	....
Eyes	....	....

Week 7

Day 46: Bathroom

Sink	Vask (vask)
Toilet	Toilet (toi-let)
Shower	Bruser (bru-ser)
Bathtub	Badekar (ba-de-kar)
Mirror	Spejl (spaigel)
Towel	Håndklæde (hawn-klae-de)
Soap	Sæbe (sæ-be)
Toothbrush	Tandbørste (tan-bør-ste)
Shampoo	Shampoo (sham-poo)
Hairdryer	Hårtørrer (hawr-tør-rer)

Write the right words down twice on the next page

Mirror	....	....
Sink	....	....
Hairdryer	....	....
Shower	....	....
Bathtub	....	....
Mirror	....	....
Towel	....	....
Soap	....	....
Toothbrush	....	....
Toilet	....	....
Shampoo	....	....
Towel	....	....
Soap	....	....
Hairdryer	....	....
Sink	....	....
Toilet	....	....
Shower	....	....
Bathtub	....	....
Toothbrush	....	....
Shampoo	....	....

Week 7

Day 47: Living Room

Sofa	Sofa (so-fa)
Television	Fjernsyn (fjern-syn)
Coffee table	Sofabord (so-fa-bord)
Bookshelf	Bogreol (bog-re-ol)
Lamp	Lampe (lump-eh)
Rug	Tæppe (taep-peh)
Cushion	Pude (poo-de)
Remote control	Fjernbetjening (fjern-be-tyen-ing)
Curtains	Gardiner (gar-di-ner)
Fireplace	Pejs (pais)

Write the right words down twice on the next page

Rug ....

Sofa ....

Remote control ....

Television ....

Coffee table ....

Bookshelf ....

Lamp ....

Cushion ....

Curtains ....

Fireplace ....

Sofa ....

Television ....

Fireplace ....

Lamp ....

Rug ....

Cushion ....

Remote control ....

Curtains ....

Bookshelf ....

Coffee table ....

Week 7

Day 48: Finance

Budget	Budget (bud-get)
Savings	Opsparing (op-sparing)
Debt	Gæld (gæld)
Income	Indkomst (in-komst)
Expenses	Udgifter (ud-gif-ter)
Bank account	Bankkonto (bank-kon-to)
Credit card	Kreditkort (kre-dit-kort)
Interest	Rente (ren-te)
Loan	Lån (lawn)
Stock market	Aktiemarked (ak-tie-mar-ked)

Write the right words down twice on the next page

Savings ....

Loan ....

Debt ....

Income ....

Expenses ....

Budget ....

Income ....

Expenses ....

Interest ....

Loan ....

Stock market ....

Budget ....

Bank account ....

Credit card ....

Debt ....

Savings ....

Interest ....

Bank account ....

Credit card ....

Stock market ....

Week 7

Day 49: Books

Writer	Forfatter (for-fatter)
Page	Side (si-de)
Table of Contents	Indholdsfortegnelse (in-dhols-for-te-gnel-se)
Foreword	Forord (for-ord)
Introduction	Introduktion (in-tro-duk-tion)
Front cover	Forside (for-side)
Back cover	Bagside (bag-side)
Text	Tekst (tekst)
Title	Titel (ti-tel)
Picture	Billede (bil-le-de)

Write the right words down twice on the next page

Front cover	....	....
Table of Contents	....	....
Title	....	....
Picture	....	....
Introduction	....	....
Back cover	....	....
Page	....	....
Foreword	....	....
Title	....	....
Text	....	....
Back cover	....	....
Picture	....	....
Writer	....	....
Page	....	....
Table of Contents	....	....
Foreword	....	....
Introduction	....	....
Front cover	....	....
Writer	....	....
Text	....	....

Week 8

Day 50: Law

Witness	Vidne (vid-ne)
Justice	Retfærdighed (ret-fair-di-hed)
Judge	Dommer (dom-mer)
Victim	Offer (of-fer)
Perpetrator	Gerningsmand (gern-ings-mand)
Court	Domstol (dom-stol)
Evidence	Bevis (be-vis)
Lawyer	Advokat (ad-vo-kat)
Crime	Kriminalitet (krim-i-na-li-tet)
Government	Regering (re-ge-ring)

Write the right words down twice on the next page

Perpetrator	....	....
Court	....	....
Justice	....	....
Evidence	....	....
Victim	....	....
Government	....	....
Judge	....	....
Victim	....	....
Perpetrator	....	....
Court	....	....
Evidence	....	....
Lawyer	....	....
Crime	....	....
Government	....	....
Witness	....	....
Justice	....	....
Crime	....	....
Judge	....	....
Witness	....	....
Lawyer	....	....

More words for you

Questions	Spørgsmål	....	....
Answers	Svar	....	....
Think	Tænke	....	....
Know	Vide	....	....
Understand	Forstå	....	....
Show	Vise	....	....
Feel	Føle	....	....
Hear	Høre	....	....
Take	Tage	....	....
Give	Give	....	....
Book	Bog	....	....
Chair	Stol	....	....
Table	Bord	....	....
Telephone	Telefon	....	....
Computer	Computer	....	....
Game	Spil	....	....
Mountain	Bjerg	....	....
Forest	Skov	....	....
River	Flod	....	....
City	By	....	....
Country	Land	....	....
Sea	Hav	....	....

Sun	Sol	....	....
Moon	Måne	....	....
Man	Mand	....	....
Woman	Kvinde	....	....
Child	Barn	....	....
Family	Familie	....	....
Friend	Ven	....	....
House	Hus	....	....
Car	Bil	....	....
Work	Arbejde	....	....
School	Skole	....	....
University	Universitet	....	....
Eat	Spise	....	....
Drink	Drikke	....	....
Beer	Øl	....	....
Wine	Vin	....	....
Cheese	Ost	....	....
Big	Stor	....	....
Small	Lille	....	....
Good	God	....	....
Bad	Dårlig	....	....
Young	Ung	....	....
Old	Gammel	....	....

Beautiful	Smuk	....	....
Ugly	Grim	....	....
New	Ny	....	....
Fast	Hurtig	....	....
Slow	Langsom	....	....
Warm	Varm	....	....
Cold	Kold	....	....
Friendly	Venlig	....	....
Unfriendly	Uvenlig	....	....
Easy	Nem	....	....
Heavy	Tung	....	....
Expensive	Dyr	....	....
Cheap	Billig	....	....
Quiet	Stille	....	....
Be	Være	....	....
Have	Have	....	....
Do	Gøre	....	....
Go	Gå	....	....
Come	Komme	....	....
See	Se	....	....
Hear	Høre	....	....
Speak	Tale	....	....
Read	Læse	....	....

Write	Skrive	....	....
Eat	Spise	....	....
Drink	Drikke	....	....
Run	Løbe	....	....
Sleep	Sove	....	....
Work	Arbejde	....	....
Learn	Lære	....	....
Help	Hjælpe	....	....
Play	Spille	....	....
Search	Søge	....	....
Buy	Købe	....	....
Stay	Blive	....	....
Stand	Stå	....	....
Sit	Sidde	....	....
Carry	Bære	....	....
Meet	Møde	....	....
Leave	Forlade	....	....
Begin	Begynde	....	....
Tell	Fortælle	....	....
Win	Vinde	....	....
Lose	Tabe	....	....
Open	Åbne	....	....
Close	Lukke	....	....

Improve	Forbedre	....	....
Explain	Forklare	....	....
Follow	Følge	....	....
Remember	Huske	....	....
Forget	Glemme	....	....
Pay	Betale	....	....
Sell	Sælge	....	....
Send	Sende	....	....
Receive	Modtage	....	....
Decide	Beslutte	....	....
Visit	Besøge	....	....
Love	Elske	....	....
Hate	Hade	....	....
Celebrate	Fejre	....	....
Dance	Danse	....	....
Sing	Synge	....	....
Jump	Springe	....	....
Newspaper	Avis	....	....
Magazine	Magasin	....	....
Letter	Brev	....	....
Card	Kort	....	....
Gift	Gave	....	....
Party	Fest	....	....

Holidays	Ferier	....	....
Travel	Rejse	....	....
Photo	Foto	....	....
Camera	Kamera	....	....
Light	Lys	....	....
Art	Kunst	....	....
Culture	Kultur	....	....
History	Historie	....	....
Nature	Natur	....	....
Environment	Miljø	....	....
Weather	Vejr	....	....
Rain	Regn	....	....
Snow	Sne	....	....
Ice	Is	....	....
Fast	Hurtig	....	....
Slow	Langsom	....	....
Early	Tidlig	....	....
Late	Sen	....	....
Simple	Simpel	....	....
Difficult	Svær	....	....
Strong	Stærk	....	....
Weak	Svag	....	....
Correct	Korrekt	....	....

Wrong	Forkert	....	....
Safe	Sikker	....	....
Dangerous	Farlig	....	....
Important	Vigtig	....	....
Interesting	Interessant	....	....
Boring	Kedelig	....	....
Happy	Glad	....	....
Sad	Trist	....	....
Healthy	Sund	....	....
Sick	Syg	....	....
Tired	Træt	....	....
Animal	Dyr	....	....
Dog	Hund	....	....
Cat	Kat	....	....
Bird	Fugl	....	....
Fish	Fisk	....	....
Horse	Hest	....	....
Street	Gade	....	....
Way	Vej	....	....
Bridge	Bro	....	....
Square	Plads	....	....

Help Us Share Your Thoughts!

Dear reader,

We hope you enjoyed reading this book as much as we enjoyed making it for you. This book is part of a special collection from **Skriuwer (www.skriuwer.com)**, a global community dedicated to creating books that make language learning an engaging and enjoyable experience.

Our journey doesn't end here. We believe that every reader is part of our growing family. If there was anything in this book you did not like, or if you have suggestions for improvement, we are all ears! Do not hesitate to contact us at **kontakt@skriuwer.com**. Your feedback is extremely valuable in making our books even better.

If you enjoyed your experience, we would be thrilled to hear about it! Consider leaving a review on the website where you purchased this book. Your positive reviews not only warm our hearts, but also help other language learners to discover and enjoy our books.

Thank you very much for choosing **Skriuwer**. Let's continue to explore the wonders of languages and the joy of learning together.

Warm regards,
The Skriuwer Team

Printed in Great Britain
by Amazon

Learn 10 Danish Words a Day for 7 Weeks

In this book, language learning becomes an enjoyable experience as you explore the wonders of Danish vocabulary. With a unique approach of learning 10 words per day, you'll be amazed at how quickly your language skills flourish. From everyday objects to essential phrases, each word is carefully selected to provide a strong foundation for your Danish language journey.

Key Features:

Efficient Learning Method: This book introduces a systematic approach of learning 10 Danish words per day for 7 weeks. By focusing on a manageable number of words each day, you'll gradually build a rich vocabulary without feeling overwhelmed.

Perfect for Children and Beginners: With user-friendly explanations, interactive exercises, and captivating illustrations, this book is tailored to meet the needs of young learners and those new to the Danish language. It provides an ideal starting point for anyone eager to explore the Danish-speaking world.

Linking English and Danish: Each word is presented with its English translation, allowing you to effortlessly make connections between the two languages. Strengthen your comprehension and expand your linguistic skills as you master the essential vocabulary.

ISBN 9798851308024

9 798851 308024

90000